CAMILA CABELLO

POP AND R&B SINGER

KATIE LAJINESS

Big Buddy Books
An Imprint of Abdo Publishing
abdobooks.com

BIG BUDDY **POP** BIOGRAPHIES

abdobooks.com

Published by Abdo Publishing, a division of ABDO, PO Box 398166, Minneapolis, Minnesota 55439.
Copyright © 2019 by Abdo Consulting Group, Inc. International copyrights reserved in all countries.
No part of this book may be reproduced in any form without written permission from the publisher.
Big Buddy Books™ is a trademark and logo of Abdo Publishing.

Printed in the United States of America, North Mankato, Minnesota.
102018
012019

Cover Photo: Nicholas Hunt/Getty Images.
Interior Photos: Boston Globe/Getty Images (p. 9); Chip Somodevilla/Getty Images (p. 15);
    Christopher Polk/Getty Images (p. 29); David Becker/Getty Images (p. 5); Dimitrios Kambouris/
    Getty Images (p. 21); Frazer Harrison/Getty Images (p. 11); Ian West/PA Wire/AP Images (p. 23);
    Jason Merritt/Getty Images (p. 13); Kevin Winter/Getty Images (pp. 19, 25); Mario Tama/Getty
    Images (p. 27); Nicholas Hunt/Getty Images (p. 6); Theo Wargo/Getty Images (p. 17).

Coordinating Series Editor: Tamara L. Britton
Contributing Series Editor: Jill M. Roesler
Graphic Design: Jenny Christensen, Cody Laberda

Library of Congress Control Number: 2018948442

Publisher's Cataloging-in-Publication Data

Names: Lajiness, Katie, author.
Title: Camila Cabello / by Katie Lajiness.
Description: Minneapolis, Minnesota : Abdo Publishing, 2019 | Series: Big buddy
    pop biographies set 4 | Includes online resources and index.
Identifiers: ISBN 9781532117985 (lib. bdg.) | ISBN 9781532171024 (ebook)
Subjects: LCSH: Cabello, Camila, 1997- (Karla Camila Cabello Estrabao)--
    Juvenile literature. | Singers--Biography--Juvenile literature. | Popular music--
    Juvenile literature. | Musicians--Biography--Juvenile literature.
Classification: DDC 782.42164092 [B]--dc23

CONTENTS

AMAZING SINGER

Camila Cabello is a gifted singer. Many know her for her **pop** and **R&B** music. She is a past member of the music group Fifth Harmony. Then she started a successful **solo** act.

Throughout her **career**, Camila has had many hit singles. And she has won several music **awards**. Camila's fans see her as a **role model**.

SNAPSHOT

NAME:
Karla Camila
Cabello Estrabao

BIRTHDAY:
March 3, 1997

BIRTHPLACE:
Cojímar, Cuba

POPULAR ALBUMS:
Camila (solo), *Better Together* (EP), *Reflection*, *7/27* (with Fifth Harmony)

FAMILY TIES

Camila's full name is Karla Camila Cabello Estrabao. She was born in Cojímar, Cuba, on March 3, 1997.

Her parents are Alejandro Cabello and Sinuhe Cabello Estrabao. Camila has a younger sister named Sofia.

Camila's sister Sofia cheered for Camila at the 2018 Grammy Awards.

WHERE IN THE WORLD?

GULF OF
MEXICO

Florida
UNITED STATES

ATLANTIC
OCEAN

THE BAHAMAS

Cojímar

CUBA

ISLA DE LA
JUVENTUD

**CAYMAN ISLANDS
(UNITED KINGDOM)**

CARIBBEAN
SEA

JAMAICA

HAITI

EARLY YEARS

When she was six years old, Camila and her mother **immigrated** to the United States. They settled in Miami, Florida. More than a year later, Camila's father traveled from Mexico. Finally, they lived together as a family again.

DID YOU KNOW?

When she first moved to the United States, Camila did not speak English. So she watched cartoons to help her learn the language.

Camila did not make it into her school's choir when she first tried out. But she made it into the singing club the next year.

THE X FACTOR

For Camila's fifteenth birthday, she wanted to try out for *The X Factor*. She was nervous. It was her first time singing in front of people. Luckily, the judges loved her **performance**!

DID YOU KNOW ?

Camila and her mom drove from Miami to Greensboro, North Carolina, for *The X Factor* tryouts.

Camila's Fifth Harmony bandmates were *(from left)* Lauren Jauregui, Normani Kordei, Ally Brooke, and Dinah Jane Hansen.

The judges asked Camila to join a singing group with four other women. The group was Fifth Harmony. The band placed third on *The X Factor*. For their last song on the show, Fifth Harmony sang "Let It Be" by the Beatles.

DID YOU KNOW ?
Fifth Harmony was the group's third name. They were first called LYLAS and then 1432.

After the show, judge Simon Cowell offered the group a record deal.

FIFTH HARMONY

    As soon as the show ended, Fifth Harmony joined singer Cher Lloyd on tour. Shortly after, the group **released** an **EP** called *Better Together*. It came out at number six on the *Billboard* albums chart. It sold 28,000 copies in the first week!

Fifth Harmony performed at the White House during the 2015 Easter Egg Roll.

The women continued their rise to fame by **releasing** a full album called *Reflection*. It came out in 2015.

Their next album was called *7/27*. It was a hit! The single "Work From Home" reached number four on the *Billboard* Hot 100 music chart.

Despite Fifth Harmony's fame, Camila wanted to make her own music. So she went **solo** in 2016.

Camila also plays guitar and writes music. She sometimes makes videos of herself playing her own songs.

SOLO CAREER

After leaving Fifth Harmony, Camila worked hard on her **solo** album. Singer Sia helped Camila with her first single, "Crying in the Club." And Pharrell Williams **produced** the song "Havana." It went to number one on the *Billboard* Hot 100 chart.

In 2015, Camila sang a hit song with pop star Shawn Mendes. "I Know What You Did Last Summer" was on the *Billboard* Hot 100 music chart for 20 weeks.

Before she **released** her first album, Camila appeared on many TV shows. She sang "Havana" on *The Tonight Show Starring Jimmy Fallon*. She also **performed** the song on the talk show *Today*.

DID YOU KNOW

Camila loves to read. Her favorite book is *The Book Thief* by Markus Zusak. She also likes to read poetry.

Her self-titled album *Camila* sold 119,000 copies in its first week.

A VOICE FOR OCD

Camila has **obsessive-compulsive disorder (OCD)**. But she does not let the illness get her down. Camila speaks openly about living with OCD. Now other people look up to Camila as a **role model**.

DID YOU KNOW?
In the United States, one in every 100 children has OCD.

Some people with OCD wash and clean too much. Others check and re-check if something is closed or locked.

AWARDS

Camila went to many **award** shows in 2018. She brought her mother to the **Grammy Awards** as her date.

She took home the FanGirls Award at the iHeartRadio Music Awards. She also won the 2018 Teen Choice Award for Choice Female Artist.

Camila shared her immigration story at the 2018 Grammys. She said that immigrants deserve a chance to make it in America.

GIVING BACK

Camila has given back to many good causes. She has worked with groups that help kids receive health care and education.

In 2016, Camila partnered with Save the Children. She made "Love Only" T-shirts to help raise money for the cause. She was **inspired** by Save the Children's **mission** to give kids a better **future**.

Camila joined many stars to sing "Almost Like Praying." All money made from song sales went to help people in Puerto Rico after hurricane Maria.

BUZZ

Throughout 2018, Camila traveled around the world. From May to October, she was the opening act on Taylor Swift's world tour.

That year, Camila continued to **release** new songs. She is one of the world's most popular artists. Fans are excited to see what Camila does next!

Camila performed alongside Taylor Swift *(center)* and Charli XCX *(right)* during Taylor's 2018 tour. The three sang Taylor's song "Shake It Off."

GLOSSARY

award something that is given in recognition of good work or a good act.

career work a person does to earn money for living.

EP extended play. A music recording with more than one song, but fewer than a full album.

future (FYOO-chuhr) a time that has not yet occured.

Grammy Award any of the awards given each year by the National Academy of Recording Arts and Sciences. Grammy Awards honor the year's best accomplishments in music.

immigrant someone who has left his or her home and settled in a new country. To immigrate is to leave one country to settle in a new one.

inspire to move someone to act, create, or feel emotions.

mission a task that is regarded as a very important duty.

obsessive-compulsive disorder (OCD) excessive thoughts that lead to repeated behaviors.

perform to do something in front of an audience. A performance is the act of doing something, such as singing or acting, in front of an audience.

pop relating to popular music.

produce to oversee the making of a movie, an album, or a radio or television show.

R&B a form of popular music that features a strong beat. It is inspired by jazz, gospel, and blues styles.

release to make available to the public.

role model a person who other people respect and try to act like.

solo a performance by a single person.

ONLINE RESOURCES

Booklinks
NONFICTION NETWORK
FREE! ONLINE NONFICTION RESOURCES

To learn more about Camila Cabello, visit **abdobooklinks.com**. These links are routinely monitored and updated to provide the most current information available.

INDEX